Shachuna's
Thoughts
about
Chakras

Mary Funkhouser

Shachuna's Thoughts about Chakras

Using Essential Oils and Other Tools from Mother Earth for Spiritual Growth

ISBN: 978-0692390535

Printed in the USA

Publishing Services
DMBookPro.com

The Chakras

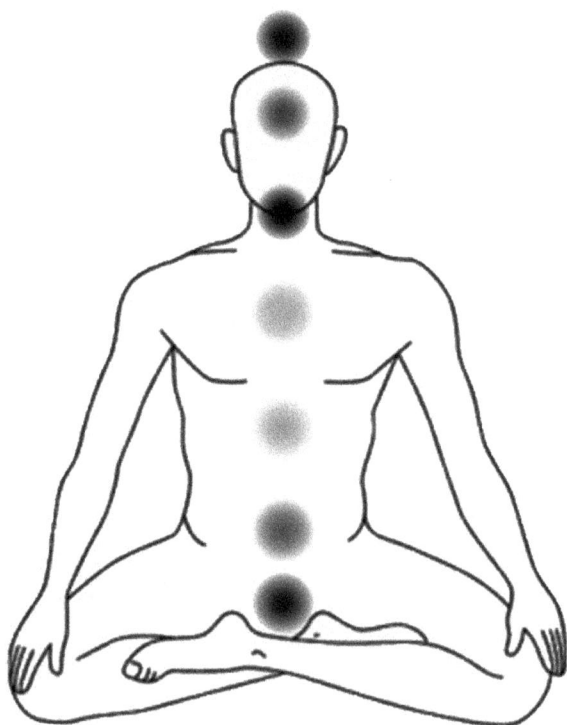

Contents

INTRODUCTION

*W*hat is a chakra? The word chakra is a Sanscrit word for wheel, meaning "energy centers" or "circular power." The chakras hold the individualized energies, attributes and qualities of the Creator. They are referred to as the "mind centers" of the physical body. When these mind centers are balanced, they work together in harmony which results in self-mastery. When they are out of balance, they create discord, "dis-ease" and chaos which results in struggle and strife.

But lately I am reading more how they are affecting our growth and our ascension process.

Our chakra is our gateway to expression of the Creator's universe, it is our source of spiritual and energy it enables a constant flow of the Creator's light to support our existence in oneness with the Creator. Our chakras are continuously altering and evolving, even their purpose can change as the vibration of energy within and around us heightens.

Our chakras are personal to us and act as a personal connection and expression of the Creator through us. Sometimes we experience blockages in certain chakras this can be the area in which our connection with the Creator needs to be address.

Each chakra relates to various glands in our body. Various colors affect them. Sound is another. Essential oils can open and help keep them in balance. Our thoughts also help control.

There are 7 chakras within our physical body with more expanding. We do have a total of 5 more we are able to access now and many more that we will have access to.

There are many benefits to chakra work, with the most obvious one the progression on our path of enlightened that we will feel. What this really means is that when our chakras are aligned, our lives is simply better, our emotional center is better, we sleep better, and we may even be getting more psychic information than we ever thought possible There are so many benefits to chakra work.

While it is important to align our chakras for balance, healing, and a more enlightened life, you don't need to look at the entire picture all at once. You don't even need to work with every chakra at once. If you just want to tweak something in your life like, maybe your intuitive growth, or maybe your sexual lifestyle, chakra work is all you need to do in order to make that magic happen. But you never need to work all 7 at once, unless you want to and have that kind of time. You just work with whatever one you want to work on, and come back to the others another time.

A word of caution: in using essential oils to remember they are very concentrated plant material (1 drop almost equal 40 cups of tea). When using oils just select a few or one to work with. In putting them directly on your body, always use a carrier oil such as almond oil. Another way is to put oils on palm of hand rub hands together in clockwise direction smell and then place near the Chakra and breathe the oils in through the chakra.

For my blends, I used Young Living Oils as my blended oils. You can find out more about the oils from www. ShachunasThoughts.com

One

1st Chakra - Root

The root chakra is our foundation and feeling grounded. It is our passion for life, intuition and our connection to Earth. Issues associated with this chakra includes personal safety, personality stability and grounded. To be here in the now, it is our survival center and our self-preservation.

We integrated the attributes and virtues of the Creator, which was infused into the seven chakras of our physical vessel and which are the dominant energies of our solar system.

We need to look at our root chakra to see what we must release in order to return to harmony with this world which focuses on strength, power, abundance, will and courage.

Are we carrying residual energies of anger and scarcity? Are we still functioning in a survival mode? Are we afraid to use our will to claim our power? We need to let go of all the negative energies that are keeping us from claiming our birthright of abundance, love, and joy.

Location: The root chakra is the energy center right at the end of our tailbone, on our bottom. It is important to our feeling of security, and for our feeling of basic safety. If we are feeling fearful about something, closing our eyes and thinking about the color red will help. Wearing red helps.

Gland: This chakra's corresponding gland is the Adrenal gland. If we have an issue with this gland then we need to work with the root chakra. Situated on top of each kidney in the lower back, at the level of lower ribs. It is the strongest gland in the body, producing hormones (including adrenaline) secreted under stress to prepare for "fight or flight" response.

Color: The color for the root chakra is magenta or red with blue/violet this is changing as we are changing with our vibration. The body mind spirit has a subtle way of telling us what we need to bring ourselves into balance. Often, we find a need to wear a certain color, we are receiving a message that the chakra in that color predominates needs a little support.

Sound: The sound for the root chakra is UH (huh).

Stones: Stones to use are Hematite, Black Tourmaline, Red Jasper, Garnet, Ruby or Bloodstone. Another stone is Aragonite. This is a strong stone to heal the earth and to heal us both emotionally and spiritually. It resonates strongly through the base chakra and the earth chakra to release excess energy and spiritual grounding into Mother Gaia. The vibration of these stones aids us to feel a stronger sense of support and connection to the earth. The energy of Aragonite Star Cluster will balance and support our lower chakras and provide us with a feeling of stability in our life.

Essential oils: To use for opening and balancing the root chakra. To find out more about these oils go to www.ShachunasThoughts.com

Ginger
Cypress
Sandalwood
Valor
Abundance
Grounding

Mix 1 drop of Ginger, Cypress, and Sandalwood with carrier oil, then rub on the root chakra. Then use the blended oils and apply where suggested.

Valor was formulated to help empower the physical and spiritual bodies. It helps overcome fear and opposition so we can stand tall during adversity. It may help build courage, confidence, and self-esteem. It brings a feeling of calmness, peace and relaxation.

It has been found beneficial in helping to align the physical structure of the body; relieves pain along spine. It also balances and align electrical energies within the body. It is best applied with 6 drops on bottom of each foot . *Put Valor on heart, Throat Chakra, wrist, solar plexus from neck to thymus. To balance left and right brain, put Valor on left fingers and rub on right temple, put on right finger and rub on left temple.*

Abundance is a formula that was specifically created to help enhance magnetic energy and create the law of attraction through the magnetic field around us, to enhance our thoughts through electrical stimulation and the cells to put out a frequency charge of prosperity and abundance. *Place on wrist, behind ears, neck and face.*

Grounding was developed to help stabilize and ground us in order to deal logically with reality in a peaceful manner. Sometimes we disconnect from reality either because we are excited about new ideas or want to escape into a protective fantasy. Our escape makes it too easy to make choices that lead to unfortunate circumstances. Grounding should help us deal with reality. *Wear on the back of the neck and on temples.*

Balanced: With a balanced Root Chakra we can feel grounded, master of oneself, can manifest abundance, and have limitless energy.

Notes

Two

2ND CHAKRA - SACRAL

This is where our spiritual-desired body was aligned with the mental, emotional and physical aspects of our Being. It is where the energies of desire, sexual/passionate love, emotions and our instinctual nature are stored in the physical body, the area in which the ego-desire body has ruled for so long. See all the stored energies of the ego-desire body (which is never satisfied), jealousy, envy, over indulgence and addiction, being transmuted. The sacral chakra is our connection and ability to accept others and new experiences. It is a sense of abundance, well-being, pleasure and being sexual. This chakra is good for helping you iron out emotional problems, whether they are big life transforming ones or ones that just muck your day. The sacral is probably the least chakra that is given much recognition about its true meaning. The energy of this chakra is about sacred sexuality which was our God given ability when we were breathed forth. We have been taught that sex was dirty or only for procreation or not talked about at all. We don't know how having an orgasm will take us in direct contact with God.

Location: The placement for this chakra is in our lower abdomen, about 2 inches below the navel.

Gland: The glands associated with the Sacral is Gonads/Sexual organs.

Color: The color for the naval chakra is pink/orange. If you are feeling down in the dumps, a little bit of orange in your day will help to inject some alignment into your sacral chakra. This color is good for confidence and will help you to relate to other people around you in friendly and helpful ways, thus boosting your confidence up even more.

Sound: The sound ooo (you) is a toning sound to enhance the sacral chakra.

Stones: Stones best to use are Carnelian, Rutilated Quartz, Amber, Citrine.

Essential oils:

Clary Sage
Rosewood
Patchouli
Peace and Calming
Harmony
Inner Child
Forgiveness

Mix 1 drop of Clary Sage, Rosewood, Patchouli and Harmony to carrier oil and apply to sacral energy center. Peace and Calming, Inner Child, and Forgiveness could be mixed together and apply to sacral chakra or apply individually.

Peace and Calming were formulated to reduce depression, anxiety, stress and tension. It may be useful at the end of a stressful day to bring about relaxation, peace, or to relieve insomnia. *Apply under nose, back of neck and feet.*

Harmony was design for us to be in harmony with ourselves, our creator, others, and the world around us before we can truly feel and overcome our negative emotions. When we have harmony in our lives, many other things will come to balance and fruition. It may promote physical, and emotional healing, by bringing about harmony balance to the sacral chakras which allows feeling of well being. It unlocks the sacral chakra. *Blend this with single oils and apply to the sacral chakra.*

Inner Child has a fragrance that may stimulate memory response and help one reconnect with their inner self or own identity, which is one of the first steps to finding emotional balance. When children have been abused and misused, they become disconnected from their inner child, or identity, which causes confusion. This can contribute to multiple personalities. These problems may not manifest themselves until early to mid-adult years, often labeled as mid-life crisis. *Apply around navel and nose.*

Forgiveness was formulated to help people move past the barriers in life. It brings them into a higher spiritual awareness of their needs, which leaves an angelic feeling in their soul that raises their frequency to the point where they feel almost compelled to forgive, forget, let go, and go on with their lives. *Massage over the navel, heart, behind the ears and on the wrist.*

Balance: When the sacral chakra is balanced we are creative, friendly, attuned to feelings, intuitive, and have concern for others.

Notes

Notes

Three

3RD CHAKRA - SOLAR PLEXUS

The solar plexus is the center of personal power, our ability to be confidence and in-control of our lives. Will and determination are governed by the third chakra. It is here that we often receive messages that alert us to danger or fraudulence. We say that we had a "gut feeling" about this or that and that feeling guided our decisions. Humanity does not know that eon of time ago an implant was put in our etheric body of our solar plexus when we fell from grace. More about this in the heart chakra.

Location: The solar plexus chakra is located on the solar plexus of our body, which is on the breastbone just behind our abdomen.

Gland: The gland associated with the solar plexus is the pancreas.

Color: Yellow energy which we carry in the third chakra or solar plexus is our emotional/personal power center, self-control, sense of authority and where, in unison with the heart, we project love/light. See this yellow radiate a brilliant gold color to this chakra as we release all negative attachments and clear the emotional trauma, all the psychic energy we have absorbed from others down through the ages, as well as all the hurt, anger and fear. How does it feel to take back our authority, self-control and to project only love and light out into the world.

Sound: The sound for this chakra is OH (GO).

Stones: Stones to use are topaz, citrine, tiger's eye.

Essential Oils:

Fennel
Juniper
Lemongrass
Harmony
En-R-Gee
Acceptance
Release
Sacred mountain

Mix 1 drop of Fennel, Juniper, Lemongrass and Harmony mixed with a carrier oil and apply to the solar plexus. Then use the blended oil and apply where suggested.

En-R-Gee oil was formulated to help improve one's energy in a natural way without over stimulating or creating problems that may be uncomfortable. It may help with mental alertness. *Apply on wrist, and behind ears, Massage across base of neck, and temples.*

Acceptance was formulated to help stimulate the mind to open up and accept new things in life, which enable one to reach toward their potential. It is to help people overcome procrastination and denial and to create a feeling of security. *Rub over liver (when the liver is toxic, the mind and emotions are lethargic), chest, face, heart, neck, and wrist. Diffuse for great results.*

Release was formulated with the objective of enhancing the release of memory trauma from the cells of the liver, which stores anger and hate emotions. The frequency of the oils in release may aid in the letting go of negative emotions so one can progress in a more effective and efficient way. It helps release frustration. *Apply over the liver, put on ears, bottom of feet.*

Sacred Mountain creates a feeling of protection, empowerment, and grounding. It helps one find security and sacredness within oneself. In addition, it is anti-bacterial and is soothing to the respiratory system. *Apply to the solar plexus, brain stem, crown of the head, back of the neck, behind ears, thymus, and wrist.*

Balance: In a balanced state you are powerful, confident, and successful in all your ventures.

Notes

Four

4TH CHAKRA - HEART

The Heart Chakra is our ability to love. This is our solar power/bridge to the upper chakra. This is our center for spirituality and compassion, and our energy center that engages and receive unconditional love. When this center is out of whack, we don't love anybody, and mostly don't love ourselves, and it is literally caused by a broken heart. Our fall from Grace many eons of years ago we closed our Heart Chakra. We believe we would no longer feel the painful effects of the negative things we were creating through the misuse of our thoughts, feeling words, and actions. When we closed our Heart Chakra, we blocked the portal through which our Mother God's Divine Love entered our lives and the physical plane of Earth. That caused our right-brain hemisphere to become almost dormant and our spiritual brain centers to almost close which, in turn, forced our Crown Chakras of enlightenment, wisdom, and understanding to close. That is when we lost Christ Consciousness and the ability to communicate with our I-AM-Presence and the company of Heaven. We developed fragmented and fear base human egos that became pawns to the forces of imbalance and the negative influence of the Beings referred to in ancient texts as cosmic evil. These forces realized that without the influence and balance of our Mother God's Love, Humanity would be easily manipulated and controlled to do their work. They convince our human egos into receiving an implant in the solar plexus of our etheric bodies would accelerate our spiritual growth, but that was a trick. The implant was a form of technology that prevented us from remembering the existence of our Mother God. It blocked us from reopening our Heart Chakra to a full breadth, so we could receive the full momentum of the Divine Feminine and our Mother God's Love.

Since our human egos agreed to receive this negative implant through our own free will choice, we alone were responsible for removing it. But now all that has changed. The influxes of Light that occurred during the Spring of 2014, Humanity reached a greatly accelerated frequency of 5th-Dimensional Crystalline Solar Light through the Divine Alchemy that is taking place in our physical, etheric, mental, and emotional bodies. This frequency of Light, at long last, enabled our I AM Presence to work with Mother Mary and the Company of Heaven to remove the implants from our Etheric Bodies. Mother Mary Placed a miniature Etheric Sun within the wound in every person's Etheric Body where the implant had been removed. This Sun pulsates with the Twelve 5th-Dimmensional Crystalline Solar Aspects of Deity associated with the New Earth. After the implants were removed they were encapsulated in Archangel Michael's Ring Pass Not of God's First Cause of Perfection, in preparation for the time when they would be escorted into the Heart of the Great Central Sun. This Healing was God victoriously accomplished for every man, woman, and child belonging to or serving the Earth at this time whether he or she was in or out of embodiment. On September 11, 2014 at the 28th Annual World Congress on Illumination Archangel Michael escorted into the Heart of Love in the Great Central Sun the precious Life energy that the forces of imbalance and cosmic evil had distorted into the gross mutations of the implants. The embrace of our Mother God's Transfiguring Divine Love, every particle and wave of Life that mutated into the negative implants was transmuted back into its original perfection by the Violet Flame. That awesome event cleared the way for the miraculous influxes of Light that changed the course of history. This is occurring in perfect alignment with each person's Divine Plan and the highest good for all concerned.

Location: The heart chakra is located upper middle of the the chest, below the thyroid gland and above the heart.

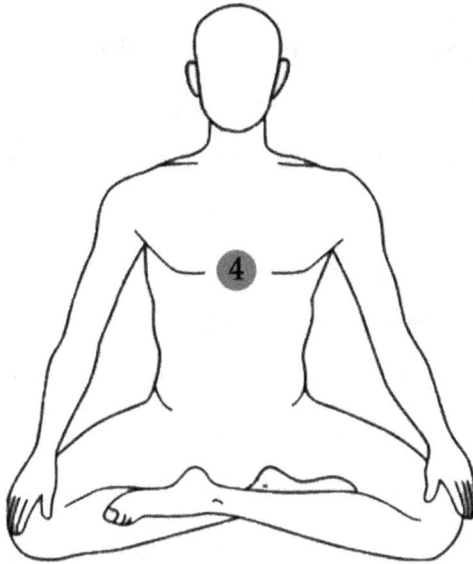

Gland: The gland corresponding to the heart is the thymus. That is why the heart chakra has expanded to include the thymus. This is called the upper heart chakra. It produces lymphocytes and antibodies for the immune system.

Color: Green is believed to be the color of the heart chakra. Many people have a pink, or sometimes pink heart chakra.

Sound: Ah (Father)

Stones: The rose quartz is the best stone to use for healing the heart Jade and emerald are good also for the heart chakra. Use Unakite if you are ready to make sustainable life changes and to heal big patterns related to health and emotional well-being. Unakite is composite of pink Feldspar, red Jasper, and green Epidote. The colors range from moss to pistachio green entwined with pink, peach, and faint red. These colors are related to the heart chakra in the proper balance. Due to the Epidote content in Unakite, it is a stone that can facilitate growth and expansion. It is a perfect stone for those who are in a committed romantic partnership, as it will expand the love and support the relationship as it matures.

Essential Oils: For the heart chakra use:

Rose
Jasmine
Ylang Ylang
Joy
Acceptance
Humility

Mix 1 drop of Rose (with rose being so expensive I use a blend that I mix with Jojoba oil), *Jasmine, and Ylang Ylang in a carrier oil and apply to heart chakra. Then apply the blends where suggested.*

Joy creates a beautiful complimentary blend of oils. When inhaled, it brings back memories of being loved, being held, sharing loving times, feeling and opening those blocks in our lives where perhaps we've shut down to love or receiving to love or love of self. When there is grief, the adenoids, and the adrenals shut down; Joy opens these glands. *Apply over heart, ears, neck, thymus, heart chakra, temples, across brow and waist.*

Acceptance was formulated to help stimulate the mind to open up and accept new things in life, which enables one to reach higher potentials. It is to help people overcome procrastination and denial and to create a feeling of security. *Rub over liver (when the liver is toxic, the mind and emotions are lethargic), chest, face, heart, neck, and wrist. Apply to sacral charka.*

Humility in having humility and forgiveness help us heal, ourselves and our earth. It is an integral ingredient in having forgiveness and seeking a closer relationship with God. Through its frequency and fragrance, we may find that special place where our own healing may begin. *Rub over the heart, on neck, temples.*

Balanced: With a balanced Heart Chakra we have unconditional love. We are balanced emotionally, empathetic, and compassionate.

Notes

Notes

Five

5TH CHAKRA-THROAT

The Throat Chakra is the most important area at this time. Many of us are experiencing stress or symptoms of discomfort here. That is because it is the power center of the spoken word, communication, discernment, and self-expression. Too long have we allowed others to decide what would be our truth, and feared to speak our truth. It is time to take back our power and to speak with honor and integrity with compassion and wisdom. It is all the impacted energies and restrictions which have kept us from speaking our truth, the dark energies of ignorant, words of judgment and criticism reside in the throat-center chakra. Communication, self expression of feeling, the truth.

Location: Is in the throat center.

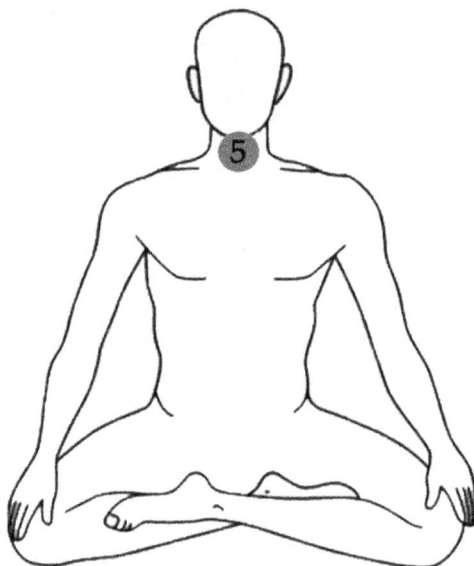

Gland: associated with the Throat Center is the thyroid/para-thyroid. It secretes hormones that regulate metabolism, particularly, those that cause rapid mobilization of fats, controls basal metabolic rate, and during childhood affects growth. Is activated by anterior pituitary gland.

Color is Deep Blue-Violet

Sound is Eye (I)

Stones: best for aligning the Throat Chakra is Aquamarine and Azurite, Sodalite and Turquoise are good stones to use.

Essential oils to use:

Bergamot
Tea Tree
Chamomile
Believe
Valor
Envision
Hope

Mix 1 drop Bergamot, Tea Tree, Chamomile with a carrier oil and place on the throat chakra. Then apply the blends were suggested.

Hope has the ability to help support the body physically and mentally in giving us hope. These oils, when inhaled together, may give us the feeling going forward with hope and achievement. It reconnects us with a feeling of strength and grounding. *Apply on ears (outer edge). It may also be placed on the chest, heart, temples, solar plexus, across the nape of neck (in back), feet, wrist, or any place on the body.*

Valor was formulated to help empower the physical and spiritual bodies. It helps overcome fear and opposition so we can stand tall during adversity. It may help build courage, confidence, and self-esteem. It brings a feeling of calmness, peace and relaxation. It has been found beneficial in helping to align the physical structure of the body; relieves pain along spine. It also balances and align electrical energies within the body. It is best applied with 6 drops on bottom of each foot . *Put Valor on heart, Throat Chakra, wrist, solar plexus from neck to thymus. To balance left and right brain, put Valor on left* *fingers and rub on right temple, put on right finger and rub on left temple.*

Believe place it directly on the throat chakra

Envision stimulates creativity and resourcefulness, encouraging renewed faith in the future and the ability to maintain the emotional fortitude necessary to achieve goals and dreams. Sometimes in life, for a variety of reasons, people suppress their internal drive. Envision helps awaken and renew that drive to overcome fear and begin experiencing new, more rewarding dimensions. *Apply two drops on wrists or temples.*

Balanced you are a good speaker, artistic, centered, live in the now, easily experience divine energy.

Notes

Six

6TH CHAKRA-THIRD EYE

*H*ere is where we integrated our intuition, clairvoyance, telepathic skills and wisdom, the gifts of Spirit you would need to function in the physical world. Here the light packets of higher wisdom and our divine Blueprint were prepared to be encoded at a later time into our brain structure. All the impacted energies stored in this chakra; fear, tension, inability to concentrate and bad dreams dissolve and turn into brilliant golden-white light as we tap into our wisdom, intuition, and telepathic skills, thereby the third eye chakra has traditionally been thought of as the portal to inner vision and communication with other dimensions, the spirit realm, and the Focus inner sight though by strengthening the bridge to our Divine-I-Am-Presence. The third eye lets you see it all. Well, not all of it, but just a little bit more. If this chakra is not balanced, you may experience headaches, or feel like we are a little afraid of being successful. You may even experience blurry vision or a strain on the eyes. The third eye is the conduit that taps into Source for the great ideas that have moved mankind forward in every field. It is through this chakra, therefore, that we can fall prey to chaos unless our head and heart are in balance. You will know this chakra is balanced when you feel like you are picking up information, but not sure where it is coming from. You may even experience telepathy or astral body work.

Location: It is located in the area of the forehead between the brow. It functions just like a third eye.

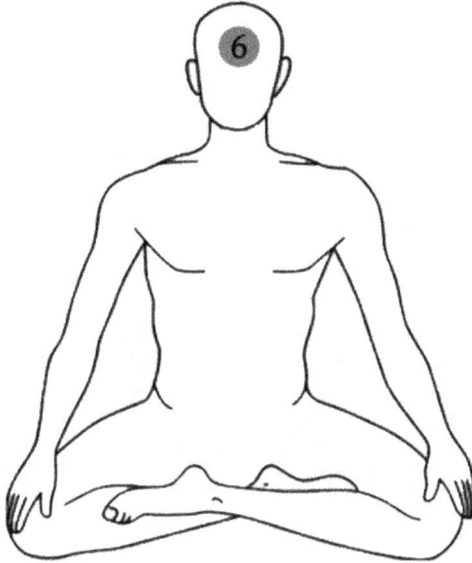

Gland: associated with third eye chakra is the pituitary gland. This governs endocrine system, as directed by the hypothalamus, anterior lobe secretes hormones regulating function of thyroid, gonads, and adrenal cortex (consequently), of vital important to growth, maturation, and activates cholesterol production to increase hormone levels.

Color: Indigo/Navy meditating on these colors will help us to align our third eye chakra.

Sound: Aye (say)

Stones Amethyst and Lapis Lazuli are famous for helping with third eye chakra alignment.

Essential Oils:

Patchouli
Cedarwood
Lavender
Awaken
Dream Catcher
Transformation
White Angelic

Mix 1 drop of Patchouli, Cedarwood, Lavender, and Transformation with carrier oil and apply to third eye chakra. Then apply the blends as suggested

Awaken this blend will awaken ourselves to the possibility of our higher potential, that we may make the necessary transitions in our lives to achieve greater things. Awaken may be beneficial and or emotional enhancement. *Apply on chest, heart. forehead, neck, temples, and wrist.*

Dream Catcher is an oil that was created to open the mind, to enhance dreams, to help one visualize and hang on to their visions or dreams until they become reality. It may also serve to protect one from negative dreams that might steal one's vision. *Rub on forehead (3rd eye area brow chakra), eyebrows, temples, behind ears, and throat chakra (base of the neck).*

Transformation these powerful oils empower you to replace negative beliefs with uplifting thoughts, changing your overall attitude, emotions, and behavior. *Apply to third eye chakra.*

White Angelic It is a beautiful blend created to give a feeling of being in a special place with protection around you. It is primarily to create a frequency field to ward off the bombardment of negative energy. It is an important oil to be used in emotional cleansing. It increases the Aura around the body, bringing a delicate sense of strength and protection and creating a greater awareness of one's potential. It may help with anger, depression, headaches, hemorrhoids, circulation, and lowering high blood pressure. *Apply on shoulders, crown, chest, behind ears, neck, forehead, and wrist.*

Balance: third eye chakra you are non-material, no fear, charismatic, total vision, master of oneself, telepathy.

Notes

Notes

Seven

7TH CHAKRA - CROWN

The seventh, or crown, chakra This highest Chakra represents our ability to be fully connected to spiritually. It is our connection to God and Spirit. The light of this chakra reaches up into the heavens. It is the conduit of the energy source that constitutes the primal flow through the body and into the earth, illustrating the "as above, so below". Balance in this chakra is essential to groundedness and, of course, for balance in all the chakra. We are said to have our meetings with our guides through the crown chakra. The seventh chakra is the center of our spiritual work, and of the work you need for full and true enlightenment. From the universe through your crown and into your soul is where wisdom and information flows, so you can imagine how psychic you would be if you had this chakra fully aligned and activated. There is a silver cord between our crown chakra and our aura body, so if you work long enough on this chakra, you can experience astral projection or out of body experiences.

Location: Seventh chakra is at the top of the head.

Gland: Is the pineal. Synthesizes and release Melatonin. Activated by sunlight. Body's "receiver" for intuition.

Color: Is white moving toward lavender, and the light of this chakra reaches up into the heavens. The blending of the Blue color of the Father Creator's will and power, and the pink of the Mother Creator's love and compassion, resulting in a lovely violet color, or the Violet Energy of the seventh Ray-the ray of the New Age. See all the impacted energies of confusion, depression, hesitation and lack of inspiration, and the static or distortion in your column of Light that connects, you to your Higher Self and Divinity I Am Presence being transmuted in a blazing Violet Flame, The sacred fire of freedom. It will transmute ALL the discordant energies of the past. All you have to do is invoke it and it will blaze up from your feet and surround you and fill you to overflowing with a never-ending supply of the transforming, magical energy.

Sound: for toning is om or aum.

Stones: For the crown all violet stone, amethyst, and fluorite Moonstone.

Essential Oils:

Frankincense
Myrrh
Lavender
Gathering
Inspiration
Three Wise Men

Mix 1 drop of Frankincense, Myrrh, Lavender with carrier oil and apply to crown chakra. Then apply blends where suggested.

Gathering increases oxygenation to the pineal Gland, bringing us more into a harmonic frequency to be a receptor of the communications that we desire to receive. It may help bring people together in spiritual oneness with God. It moves people in profound way. This oil should help bring not only the physical, but also the emotional and spiritual thoughts and feelings together for great focus and clarity and to prevent all the fracturing of thought energy. This helps us find a greater peace and balance. It helps to keep us focused, grounded, connected, and clear. This blend should help gather our potential for self-improvement. It is good to use when there has been a lack of sleep. It is proving to be a very powerful oil in supporting the body from outside attacks. It is an amplifier. *Apply to forehead, heart, right temple and take across to the left temple, bottom front of the neck, thymus, face, chest, and on each side near shoulders.*

Inspiration includes oils that have been combined to help enhance those that desire communication and getting closer to the Creator and enjoying the spiritual aspect of life. It relieves negative thoughts and enhances spiritual awareness. It creates a space for prayer and inner awareness during meditation and prayer. *Apply to horns (right and left sides of* *the forehead), crown, shoulders, and back of the neck.*

3 Wise Men opens crown to release emotions. It brings a sense of grounding and uplifting through memory recall. It keeps negative energy and negative emotions from reattaching to the body. *Apply to the crown of the head in a clockwise motion to create an energy of opening and releasing, followed by receiving the energy of the to fill the new void.*

Put neck, eyebrow, solar plexus, and thymus (clockwise).

Balance: You are an alchemist, no fear of death, miracle worker, open to the divine.

Notes

Notes

Eight

THE UPPER CHAKRAS

*A*s we clear and balance the seven major chakras of the physical body and begin the transition process of rebuilding the light body and our divine awareness, something magical begins to happen. the eight chakra is sometimes called the "soul star" or the link to our higher consciousness or the "rainbow bridge" of enlightenment. The vibrancy of Christ-Conscious begins to filter down into our chakra system, creating a rippling effect throughout our four-bodily systems, speeding up the process of releasing impacted thought-forms or the negative energies that we have carried for eons of time. The more we balance, harmonize and strengthen our chakra system, the more divine light substance we can absorb. Remember light, sound, and color are the energies of creation. (Christ or Christed means the pure Divine Essence of the Creator)

The five higher galactic rays are a combination of the first seven rays infused with the Christ-Light of the creator. There are even higher cosmic rays, but we will not be able to integrate or even understand these until we move into higher dimensional awareness.

We must know that CHRIST CONSCIOUSNESS is the enlightened state of consciousness we were invested with by our Father-Mother God when we were first breathed forth from the core of creation. This level of consciousness empowered us with the ability to easily communicate with our Father-Mother God I AM PRESENCE in the Realms of Illumined Truth through open heart and mind telepathic communication. In that state of consciousness, we realized the Oneness of All Life. We perpetually functioned from the Heart-centered space of Reverence for life with the Divine Intent of co-creating the highest good for all concerned with every thought, feeling, word, and action we expressed.

Chakra 8 is our energy center of divine love, of spiritual compassion and spiritual selflessness, one karmic residue, activates spiritual skills contained in the seventh chakra.

Chakra 9 is our soul blueprint (the individual's total skills and abilities learned in all the lifetimes).

Chakra 10 is divine creativity, synchronicity of life; the merging of the masculine and feminine within, unlocking of skills contained in the ninth chakra.

Chakra 11 is the pathway to the soul, the individual's ability to acquire advanced spiritual skills (travel beyond the limits of time and space, teleportation, bi-location, instantaneous of thoughts, telekinesis in some cases).

Chakra 12 is the connection to the Monadic level of divinity, advanced spiritual skills, ascension, connection to the cosmos and beyond.

Notes

ABOUT MARY FUNKHOUSER

*W*hen I turned 72 I decided I needed a life. It was amazing how spirit sold my house in two months in an area where houses were not selling well as going into winter nevertheless it sold.

I had lived in my house for 34 years. My husband made the transition to the other side almost 25 years ago. Then about 5 years later my son made the transition. In that time frame I opened a health food store and ran it for almost 13 years. I have felt like I have always been serving others and not tending to myself.

I started writing this book as a blog about four months ago. I have been following my intuition very closely and had a very strong urge to create it into a book.

Intuition has guided me to Sedona Arizona. I left my family which is scattered over Colorado and came to Sedona. Here I have met many wonderful people who has been guiding me in direction I need to accomplishment what spirit has for me.

For my blends, I used Young Living Oils as my blended oils. You can find out more about the oils from www. ShachunasThoughts.com

Notes

Notes

www.ingramcontent.com/pod-product-compliance
Lightning Source LLC
Chambersburg PA
CBHW071424040426
42445CB00012BA/1284